life, love
& everything
in between

Volume

1 Poetry to empower, enlighten
and entertain

T . M .   T H O M P S O N

Table of Contents

Balboa Press books may be ordered through booksellers or by contacting:

Balboa Press
A Division of Hay House
1663 Liberty Drive
Bloomington, IN 47403
www.balboapress.com
1 (877) 407-4847

ISBN: 978-1-9822-1461-6 (sc)
978-1-9822-1462-3 (e)

Library of Congress Control Number: 2018912744

Print information available on the last page.

Balboa Press rev. date: 10/25/2018

BALBOA
PRESS
A DIVISION OF HAY HOUSE

Author Foreword

The first poem I wrote was in 1977, but I never considered myself a poet until about 5 or 6 years later when I had written a reasonable number of poems. In those early poems the subject matter was usually something specific I wished to say to a specific individual. My intent was to Empower an individual or Enlighten them. Many of the poems I write today are meant to Empower or Enlighten the reader. In 1978 I was handed a book called "The Nature of Personal Reality" by the channeller Jane Roberts. For me, it is the most important book I have ever read as it was like coming home. From that point on I became a philosopher/metaphyscian and New Age concepts of Empowerment and Enlightenment were concepts I wanted to convey to others and many of my poems have that intent. My inspiration for a poem comes from something someone says, something I see, or hear triggers the first line. From there, the rest just flows.

A wise old man

A wise old man once said to me
Come son behold the dawn
Come quickly now behold yon sight
Come quick before it's gone.

And tell me now what thrills you
The breaking of the day
Or does the setting sun caress
Your cares and woes away.

Come tell me now which is it
To which do you respond
The blazing birth of light and warmth
Is it of this you're fond.

Or does the cool of evening
So sooth your furrowed brow
That twilight is a thing of joy
In times both then and now.

I do not understand wise one
Why of these must I choose
Must I be so possessed by one
The other I must lose.

Are not the joys of life then
But servants to the will
To come forth as are beckoned
And so each life to fill

Ah yes from in the child
The Master does emerge
And in so now discovering
Your limits do you purge.

For life does not require
A scale on which to weigh
The joys or pleasure one may have
On any given day.

Nowhere is it thus written
That to you it is denied
The right to taste the fruits of life
Wherever they're espied.

Remember then wherein you dwell
Contains all you desire
And naught is now beyond your reach
If you do so aspire.

So go forth now and change your world
Thus knowing what you know
And teach to others this same thing
That they too may so grow.

Forget not that to learn in life
Is but a simple task
Far harder is to answer that
Which no one yet did ask.

To speak a truth because it's true
To those who little care
Requires strength and courage
And the willingness to dare.

For often do we crucify
The seers that are born
Because their words defy our world
On them we heap our scorn.

So realize young Master
There's work indeed to do
To speak the truth and change the world
For both the world and you.

T. M. Thompson
September 16, 2011

Reincarnation

From before I can remember
I knew who I would be
And what it is I'd have to do
And what it is I'd see.

I painted me a picture
A work of art so real
That now I am a part of it
Immersed in all my zeal.

I set the stage and wrote the script
With friends and foes to aid
To counsel me and choose their parts
Ah thus the plans are laid.

But where do I find drama
Or pain or love or sorrow
If in the play no secrets wait
For me upon the morrow.

So cleverly the script is done
The play may now commence
And promptly all forget the source
And life makes little sense.

What joy so to discover
That which does now await
To bless the Gods for fortune
Or curse my life and fate.

And so it does unravel
Yet not without surprise
For that which in the mind is seen
Is different to the eyes.

For all the plans so carefully laid
And all the chosen schemes
Are images each one sends forth
To play the part of dreams.

But now the play is real
And now each author's there
And now each presence alters
The play on which they stare.

So life then is not fated
Though you do cast the theme
For when the play is carried out
T'is more than just a dream.

So love the life you've chosen
And delights that are in store
And know that what awaits you
Is not less but much, much more.

T. M. Thompson
December 8, 1978

Ten Years from now

Ten years from now you'll read these lines
With eyes that blaze anew
And wonder of the self now gone
That once you thought was you.

Crusades all but forgotten
And dramas once so real
Amaze you now that long ago
They once had such appeal.

And yet within their lifetime
They made your life worthwhile
They caused the tear upon your cheek
And made you grow and smile.

They led you to your loved ones
To treasured memories
To far off lost horizons
And to life through fantasies.

Yet though life is illusion
The gains themselves are real
The insight into who you are
And what you know and feel.

So never do forget then
The part your drama plays
Nor of the love that waits to fill
Tomorrow's, yesterdays.

T. M. Thompson
July 16, 1981

By a sapphire sea

A dark eyed beauty
By a sapphire sea
Watching the Moon
And sipping ice tea.

Tied to a desk
But her mind was quite free
To wander and dream
Of places to be.

To dream of white sand
Of Love and romance
Of a white knight with flowers
Arriving by chance.

To dream of a life
Quite different then this
Of wine and of candles
And a lover's sweet kiss.

Of a soul mate who found her
Who made life complete
For two on a journey
Who still did not meet.

But tides and your destiny
None can resist
So soon will the dream be
If you do persist.

Your future awaits you
Believe and be still
For all that you dream of
Depends on your will.

Believe and expect
Dream and make plans
And thus will your future
Be happy and grand

T. M. Thompson
July 5, 2006

Jay and Vincent van Gogh

Jay and Vincent once met in a dream
Their lives to compare and ponder
Which of us Jay do you think at this time
Did our time and our lives most squander.

My life was of science great laws did I know
Reality the test I applied
But Vincent just picked up his brush in his hand
Looked at his blank canvas and he sighed.

Shall I dear Jay upon this blank sheet
Place laws that exist or that don't
Shall I dear Jay upon this blank page
Sketch one of my dreams or a boat.

For one is quite real the other is not
Is not and may never be.
Are you then so sure that the boat does exist
And does sail on some azure blue sea.

Perhaps it's the dream known only to me
That one day will soon come to pass
Be careful dear Jay that you pause and reflect
And judge not what is true by its mass.

For the weight of ones proofs may vanish one day
Replaced by the dream you did scorn
For nothing is fixed in the world you exist
Or else you would be as when born.

The Laws of today give way to tomorrow
To the dreams that we laugh at not knowing
That things we can't prove to others are real
And will be when others start growing.

I paint using colours, red yellow and blue
For my flowers to be what they are
I paint using colours white orange and black
For the sky where I place my bright star.

In your art bright yellow are numbers that add
Greens the ones that divide
Blue to subtract and reds are a power
From which all others can't hide.

As I mix my colours you formulas build
And each does their art thus create
And one day dear Jay we'll both know the truth
About laws, about art, so let's wait.

For though we each view what's real what's not
Through beliefs that we see don't agree
In time we may find that it's you who was right
But who knows it could really be me.

T. M. Thompson
October 6, 1992

For things that are important

For things that are important
No clock may tell the time
In no ticking hand or calendar
Is reason or is rhyme.

But only by emotions
Do we hold onto what's real
The memories of joy and pain
That once we each did feel.

The day my son said daddy
My trip to a foreign land
A walk along a distant shore
The feel of the sand.

The first time that I fell in love
Those days I fell again.
The day when I discovered
To create with just my pen.

The day I met my best friend
Or a day filled with much laughter
The days in which tears filled my eyes
And the healing that came after.

Days when I was such a fool
And times when I grew wise
Days filled with a dull routine
And days with a surprise.

We watch the time intently
As each of us does know
It takes us from the place we are
To where we have to go.

But time watched is forgotten
Just the moment does remain
Whether it's of joy and love
Or everlasting pain.

So remember that those hours
Of the sweeping second hand
Are not what do determine
Why your life is oh so grand.

The times you made one smile
Or you gave a helping hand
Of happiness not sadness
Just by chance or by a plan.

These times you've now forgotten
Are the sum of who you are
That makes you like no other
And is why you are a star.

T. M. Thompson
September 3, 2004

Before a fire blazing

Before a fire blazing
Where logs to embers turn
I sit with friends so dear to me
And talk and think and learn.

Before a fire blazing
I sit in warmth and light
And ponder all the mysteries
To know what's wrong what's right.

Yet what little does it matter
The Universe to know
For here are seeds of love and joy
That in this house will grow.

So let the stars keep shining
And All That Is be so
For now my world is love and life
Before the fires glow.

T. M. Thompson
April 10, 1977

I've a hole in my shoe

I've a hole in my shoe
But nobody knows
I smile and laugh
And wiggle my toes.

Feet flat on the ground
So no one can see
They'd laugh at the hole
Known only to me.

For each of us has
A hole in their shoe
Or some part of us
We'd dread if you knew.

Yet often the hole
Is just in our head
And is nothing important
Or that we should dread.

We see in ourselves
Flaws not perfection
And expect ridicule
Aimed in our direction.

But those who love us
See with the heart not the eyes
So ignore all the fools
And pay heed to the wise.

And learn to be gentle
And know 'cause it's true
You've no hole in your soul
Nor one in your shoe.

T. M. Thompson
June 15, 2006

How strange that so much pleasure

How strange that so much pleasure
Is derived from those now dead
So many hours that I enjoy
By what they did or said.

Was there ever such an age before
Where those now gone remain
Where through their lives they come to us
To teach or entertain.

Mozart and Miller still thrill me
And Astaire who dances on air
Dorothy on her way to Oz
And the wizard living there.

Bogart still loves Bergman
As time goes slowly by
Lennon's voice still haunts me
As does Lucy in the Sky.

Diamonds still thrill Marilyn
And Hope still makes me smile
Orson's here on Halloween
They all make life worthwhile.

Shakespeare, Shelley, Keats and more
Their words I see or hear
Authors, actors, dancers, poets
Long gone are still so near.

I know it's true for each of us
We should each live in the now
And too enjoy the future
Not just to the present bow.

There's today and yes manana
But the past for me still lives
And all the joy and pleasure
Of what was that still now gives

T. M. Thompson
August 17, 2004

Sleeping Beauty 2011

Sleeping Beauty was awake last night
Her mind would not be still
For her heart yearned for her lover
But her lover had not the will.

The will to act upon his love
For to his passions he was tied
To money, drink, power and games
These kept him from her side.

The princess was young and beautiful
And only one future could she see
For her heart was for no another
Just for him and only he.

But time is just a path to where
Our destiny does await
With lessons that we each must learn
To lead us to our fate.

Cast not your pearls among the swine
And change not what won't change
But know that what you want is there
Though now that may seem strange.

For what you want is love not him
There are many you may love more
And know that this is just your path
To the happiness that's in store.

You will find love and happiness
Greater than ever you have known
It waits for you to learn the truth
Once learned you will have grown.

And the truth is that he who loves you
Fears nothing and loves nothing more.
And once you know that this is so
You'll find happiness forevermore.

T. M. Thompson
July 29, 2011

Once I was a warrior

Once I was a warrior
I lived my life to fight
I stood upon the fertile earth
With blood both left and right.

Before me lay those vanquished
While I again survived
To revel in the pleasure
From their deaths I did derive.

For killing was so easy
So many reasons came
Like race, or colour, church or state
Or just their family name.

When I was young foes sought me out
But now the roles have changed
Instead my victims do me now choose
That their death I may arrange.

But now I stand and view the corpse
I see that is my own
The fate no doubt I did deserve
From seeds myself I've sown.

Nobody here to challenge
Nor anyone to ask
If this is death then what is next
What next shall be my task.

But now in the still and quiet
Lost memories I do recall
Of other lives and other times
I now can view them all.

I see my deaths in multitude
Then what's the point to kill
If each is just reborn again
If such may be our will.

Since killing serves us not to kill
But simply end a role
Then to end a life forever so
Then cannot be our goal.

Slowly now I understand
That by such means we grow
Compassion, hate, love pain and joy
Through this we come to know.

And too we may learn tolerance
Understanding at the least
As each of us we overcome
That which in us is the beast.

And through such deaths such drama
Between foe and friend alike
Living and dying for the woman you love
Or who controls the dyke.

Though killing never can be condoned
Its purpose I understand
For it is used by souls to grow
According to their plan.

But now I've come to realize
The next step is grander still
To set aside my spear and axe
On this journey of free will.

No more a warrior shall I be
But an adventurer on a quest
To delight in all experiences
And enjoy all that is best.

So too do you come to understand
To set aside your bows
On a journey where what awaits are highs
And where there are no lows.

For wisdom need not come in death
For in life we can truly see
The pattern and the purpose of
The felling of each tree.

So from this day adventurers
Is what we both shall be
Where others play in life and death
Our journey is but to see.

To see and play, to love and laugh
To give and to receive
How wonderful my life is now
That this I now believe.

Terry Thompson
June 17, 1994

Reflections

What words would now be here
If this pen had been
In another's hand.
What thoughts
What ripples to be sent forth
To cascade in another's mind
in ways that neither could foresee
or might ever understand.
And if I had never been
or was not now
would the world cry out
against the silence.
Would not another come to fill the void
and do so in so subtle a manner
that none could detect the change
as you now
cannot detect the changes contained herein.
Yet they are there
And the rhythm and the rhyme
is no less for what it is
than for what it may have been
and your need is fulfilled
as is mine.
For each must now come to realize
that in life we do not create voids
by our absence
but do instead
fill them by our presence.
And so it is that each grows
I with pen in hand
with words to those I'll never see
and you by realizing
the many voids you fill

T. M. Thompson
September 6, 1980

Karma

Nowhere my dear in nature
Does punishment exist
Why then believe in karma
As you dear, do so persist.

There is no reward or punishment
Just adventures to undertake
To teach and learn the lessons
For ourselves and other's sake.

For each is born quite perfect
Though you may encounter strife
It is the way we choose to grow
Is why we choose this life.

For time is just illusion
Past and future are but one
There is no beginning or ending
And no finish what has begun.

There is no cause and no effect
Where time is but illusion
To focus in the here and now
Is dear the best conclusion.

No debts to pay, rewards to get
Nothing earned and nothing forgiven
Thus knowing dear you are now free
And no longer by Karma driven.

For all you want is yours dear one
You need only to accept
And the more you open to this thought
At receiving become more adept.

Believing thus the Universe
Will grant all that you ask
So open to the "All That IS"
This is your only task.

T. M. Thompson
January 13, 2010

My hand creates the written word

My hand creates the written word
In prose and flowing rhyme
Divesting each with part of me
Thrust forward into time.

To eyes that yet see nothing
And souls still yet to be
Who'll someday gaze upon these lines
And know the way of me.

For in my art I do endow
Large portions of myself
And thus in sending forth my dreams
Do I increase my wealth.

For wealth is in the knowing
That there are those who wait
For knowledge that's contained herein
By which they'll mold their fate.

For wisdom lies between the lines
You cannot see or hear
Yet all the same it still is there
Though you may think it queer.

For not all that is, is obvious
To eye, to ear, or brain
But nonetheless there's wisdom here
From which you each may gain.

For everything is energy
This poem is just a shell
Imprinted here is all I know
In words too few to tell.

Like holograms the smallest piece
Contains All that There Is
The Universe in a grain of sand
I think I'll take a wiz.

That last line is just humour
It is important that you know
To laugh and smile throughout your life
So you may learn and grow.

Don't be too serious relax don't frown
In this life that you have chosen
As you now face the challenges
Into this life you've woven.

And so I end this little rhyme
And wish you on your way
With hopes you laugh
And hopes you'll smile
Tomorrow and today.

T. M. Thompson
September 10, 1992

Little Sister from Iran

A flower in the desert
In the land of mystery
A beauty proud and noble
So far from the nearest sea.

So many see and recognize
The beauty they behold
And wish to keep the flower
From the shadows and the cold.

To nurture and encourage her
To make her laugh and smile
To help her in her journey
From the desert to the Nile.

For our flower is no flower
But a spirit that longs to soar.
To wander to new vistas
Where she=s never been before.

In a fashion she lives another=s life
And not yet one's her own.
But time and fate are on her side.
And her destiny=s well known.

One day great changes will begin
And our flower will be free
To be all of that she ever dreamed
To become what she wants to be.

T. M. Thompson
May 5, 2006

For Neda from Iran

A sunny day too nice to work

A sunny day too nice to work
So let us make a plan
We'll run away and then we'll say
O boy I'm glad I ran.

So hard to be at work again
Again there's not a gain.
For home was fun but now it's done
And work is such a pain.

Thank God for friends to make me smile
To wile away dull hours
Thank Allah, Krishna, and all the rest
For stars and seas and flowers.

For beauty feeds my inner soul
As does a coffee break
Hugs and kisses feel so good
Of these more I can take.

So slowly though I must adjust
To the pattern of my life
But soon surprise the man arrives
To take me as his wife.

So patience then for love is near
And freedom will be thine
For soon there's love and candles dear
With sweet kisses and sweet wine.

T. M. Thompson
June 21, 2006

Name Change

My name is but a vessel
Much too small for all that's me
When grown beyond its boundaries
I must surely set me free.

Like a caterpillar changes
In its form and as it's known
So it is the same with me
To show the world I've grown.

For seldom does the world perceive
The self that lies within
So symbols we can see and touch
Are how we do begin.

But symbols that we do construct
For the benefit of our peers
Are magic for in truth they are
Not just symbols, but too mirrors.

And in them lies the inner self
Upon which we may gaze
To thus connect to who we are
In each life and in each phase.

Like Cary Grant born Archie Leach
His name and life changed too
And so too for some women
When one day they said I do.

For names are just vibrations
Which many do outgrow
And so it may now be with you
By now you surely know.

That you have changed or want too
And your name now does not fit
Don't be afraid and make a change
For your life, depends on it.

T. M. Thompson
October 27, 2010

24

Heritage

A promise to my son

How many souls just like me
Have long since lost their way
How many souls live in the now
Having lost their yesterday.

Sometimes I see my heritage
In movies and on TV
And so do I regret the loss
That was my history.

The memory of my long lost roots
My grandparents place of birth
The songs the food the style of dress
To me still have great worth.

I remember grandma's cooking
And the traditions of a distant land
The songs, the dances, the way of life
I still view as so grand.

The language my grandma taught me
That now I hardly speak
So many times I think my past
Is something I should seek.

But I live in a land not of yesterdays
But of todays and of tomorrows
The culture here looks ahead not back
And such then is my sorrow.

For I live in the here and I live in the now
Neglecting all that which was
So busy am I with the day to day
For it seems this is what one does.

But memories are cherished
And do never fade away
Always there to make one smile
And to brighten a rainy day.

Who I am today I am proud of
But I want my child to know
From where it was our family came
To this country to futures sow.

New lands provide new freedoms
And too here is opportunity
To provide a better way of life
For our family for you and me.

But one's heritage should be cherished
And passed onto to those who follow
For the past is of great importance
And its meaning is never hollow.

Remember when something's transplanted
Some of the roots always stay behind
And I promise you one day we'll travel
And our heritage we both will find.

For it's always wise to retain the past
And to be proud of the fatherland
And one day soon we shall travel there
And you'll see a land quite grand.

Churches and plains, people and food
So different from where we live
Together we will share a time
In a land that has much to give.

So with this poem I promise you son
A journey you'll not regret
Of a time shared with your father
Of a time you'll not forget.

T. M. Thompson
October 18, 2010

One cent

Sometimes you're just one cent short of a dollar
And all you need is that one cent more
And sometimes all you need is just a little help
Like a helping hand or an open door.

And sometimes what's missing is encouragement
That will help you move forward to succeed
Or sometimes just a little help and support
Or a kind word is all that you need.

The difference between Gold, Bronze, or Silver
Is almost too small to measure
And too is the difference between success or failure
Or a life of pain or one of pleasure.

How often have you desperately wanted something
But just didn't quite have what was required
And all you may have needed was a gentle push
To help you move forward and be inspired.

An encouraging word or a little support
Some knowledge from your family or friend.
To be shown a path to fulfill your dream
And reach the prize at the rainbow's end.

So many times I have seen in my life
One whose dream was so near at hand
Their genius and talent was so plain to see
And too a future that could be so grand.

So whenever you can be that one cent
Be it for a stranger or for a friend
And do what you can to help them along
To the prize at the rainbow's end.

T. M. Thompson
January 8, 2013

Can you remember

Can you recall when we first met
So many lives ago
Or know you of the many times
I stood and watched you grow.

I watched you at each stage arrive
Your beauty I did behold
With love and caring I saw and smiled
And watched your path unfold.

For many times I was in your dreams
You thought I was your guide
But in truth I played so many roles
And I was often by your side.

So many different roles we played
As a way to learn or teach
In dramas where together we strove
Such lofty heights to reach.

And so many times we were apart
With different challenges to pursue
But still the best of times my love
Are the ones I shared with you.

On the path to knowing and enlightenment
On the path to becoming self-aware
On the path to where all is known
And at last we are both there.

The final stages now are reached
In this classroom, this dream, this earth
Where both have now come to understand
Our purpose, our gifts, our worth.

So now together we'll journey on
To laugh, to love, and to live
To teach, to learn, to grow, and to be
Now willing to take and to give.

Two souls now existing essentially as one
Yet each unique and themselves still apart
But sharing a common journey of joy
With each breath and each beat of the heart.

And so my darling I love you
As I have always done
And to be with you now forever
On a journey now begun.

Is heaven and always will be
Is heaven and the sky is blue
For from now until eternity
I shall always be with you.

T. M. Thompson
April 26, 2011

As You Believe

When you walk you think not of how
You think not of what you must to do
And so it is with all that you see
In the world that now surrounds you.

You need not know the how of things
You need only know the goal
For the how of things is better left
To the wisdom of your soul.

For in things unseen there is magic
That knows how to make dreams come true
And only your doubts will kill the dream
So have faith it's up to you.

So many ask for health or wealth
Believing it can't be so
But as ye believe so shall it be done
Of this I am sure you all know.

Yet so many know not just what they believe
And say why am I poor or why sick
And so they will pray to the heavens above
But their cures do seldom come quick.

For you will only accept that in which you believe
Knowing not why the answer is no.
Thinking that you're unworthy and it must be your fault
"Cause of seeds in the past you did sow.

But no thought or act denies you of love
Denies you of health or good will
Of abundance or friends or joyous adventures
Or of times pleasant quiet and still.

It's always your beliefs that will be the cause
So examine what you regard then as true
And always you'll find a yes and a no
As to why what is wanted is denied you.

I believe in abundance in wealth so I ask
For relief from this life of great lack.
But easier a camel through the eye of a needle
Than to enter heaven with gold in a sack.

So you ask then for money but regard it as evil
So then how can your prayer come to be
And so too for all other prayers there is conflict
A conflict to understand and to see.

Realize then that naught to you is denied
As to your child you would willingly give
Prosperity, health, love, peace and great joy
In this time in this place you now live.

So know that your birth right is all love can give
And nothing you want must be earned
It's you won't accept that stands in your way
I hope dear this truth you've now learned.

So open the doors to the best things in life
All life's treasure receive and to give
To others with love then share all that is good
And in happiness and love both may then live.

T. M. Thompson
March 3, 2011

The sun is gently rising

The sun is rising to start a new day
And the moon is low in the sky
Around me are friends and much beauty to see
As I watch clouds so gently pass by.

All is serene and life is a joy
Yet for what purpose do I exist
Does a destiny wait or fate rule my life
Are there futures and paths to resist.

What purpose my life, what yet to be done
Can it be just to end and be gone
Should I think not of what and think not of why
And simply enjoy each new dawn.

There are things I can't prove and things I can't know
But my beliefs hurt none and me please
Like life after death and that I create
And to none do I need bend my knees.

It pleases me to think I'm eternal
That I've a soul that always shall be
And that through each new incarnation
I will always be new but be me.

In life we will all die a thousands deaths
The child I was now since passed
The me that I am will change and be gone
For what is, is not meant to last.

The only constant is change I am told
Each day I will change and will grow
And just as my mind and body evolve
So too will my soul I do know.

In truth I know not that I do have a soul
But it pleases me and really hurts none
So why not enjoy what surrounds me
And believe in a journey begun.

A journey to become more enlightened
A journey to grow and to be
A journey to love and create things
A journey shared by you and by me.

I know much around me is tragic
But through these I will find my way
There are so many different paths to perfection
And I've a chance to find one each day.

So if I'm a fool it not matters
For I'm at peace in my life and my soul
And to be more like our source and creator
Is, and is always, my goal.

So today I will laugh and I'll smile
Today will be gentle and kind
On this path that I believe I have chosen
With my heart, with my soul, with my mind.

So I wish you well on your journey
And that all your beliefs bring you peace
For if they do not dear then change them
And all that does harm please release.

Bringing joy and bringing love then to others
May not matter if we are just dust
But to believe in a life here and hereafter
Is a choice but believe not you must.

To believe this in no way can hurt you
But you may find it eases your way
So relax, and believe and be happy
With a smile, with each breath, and each day.

T. M. Thompson
March 4, 2011

Poem with no Ending

This poem it has yet no ending
But it will because I've begun
Like life the end still not known
Nor yet has the last bell been rung.

My poem is so much like life then
We all start and hope it ends well
We dream of the joys up in heaven
Sometimes from our own personal hell.

So many think that they are victims
That no plan or a purpose does exist
No wonder they wander through life then
Unhappy and eternally pissed.

I smiled as I wrote that last line here
And suggest to you it's so good to laugh
And I hope that you also will chuckle
As I here do now practice my craft.

Not much to say or to tell you
It's just that I'm playful today
So with a wink and smile I now send you
Hopefully happily and merrily on your way.

T. M. Thompson
March 3, 2011

Persia

I've friends from far off Persia
A land quite far away
A land that I'd like to visit
And am sure I will one day.

Most what I know of Persia
Is from movies and not nearly true
It's the romantic view of a culture
With fantasy through and through.

But even in movies and Fairy Tales
There are parts that indeed are real
So one day I'll see it for myself
And do so with great zeal.

In every land there is good and bad
And there are things I'd like to change
I know of their struggles and hard times
And of their ways I find so strange.

But part of the joy of travel
Is to discover new thoughts, new ways.
And Persia has a rich proud history
And great stories of bygone days.

I know so little of its culture
But of its people I am aware
Its women so incredibly beautiful
One can only catch their breath and stare.

And the men are proud and masculine
With an inner strength and dark, dark eyes
And a way about them strong yet subtle
Which suggests they are quite wise.

So each day I really enjoy my friends
And am so glad that we all finally met
And when at last we finally do have to part
I will not them soon forget.

And I promise one day I'll visit Iran
And then I'll finally be able to see
The land that made them who they are
And then sent them off to me.

T. M. Thompson
March 10, 2011

A Little Girl Eating an Apple

A little girl eating an apple
Rosy cheeks and a hat on her head
A cherub so sweet and so innocent
Knowing nothing of what lay ahead.

A life that's the same as her mother's
With friends on a bright sunny day
With hope, and desires and so many dreams
That her children would be happy and gay.

For in Peru it is really quite common
To find many who just try to survive
By selling their wares to the tourists
Who barely know that they're alive.

For pennies they purchase a memory
Paying as little as they possibly can
Thinking little of the hardship before them
Thinking only of the view and their tan.

So those that now read what's here written
To you I suggest and do say
Pay double what they may be asking
To help brighten their life and their day.

For a tourist's life is much better
Than the child's life surely will be
Where we live amidst so much abundance
She forever lives amidst great poverty.

So I suggest then to you to be generous
Give as if the little child was your own
And know then at least for just that one day
To her you have compassion just shown.

Every act of kindness and compassion
Changes the world for more than just one
So give with a smile and a feeling
Of best wishes, of caring, and love.

T. M. Thompson
April 15, 2011

The words here are written to the tune of the song Cielito Lindo

Fields of flowers
The sun shining brightly
The wind blowing gently
I love you
My heart beating wildly
For you love
For you only

Come, come, my love
Kiss me and hold me
The sun and the flowers and the wind they all know
That I love you now and forever

Our days of magic
And days filled with love
Days that will live eternal
Days of love and devotion
Days where I whisper to you
I love you

Come, come, my love
Kiss me and hold me
The sun and the flowers and the wind they all know
That I love you now and forever.

When we first met
I knew then and there
That heaven had sent you my darling
To end this life of searching
And live happily with you forever.

Come, come, my love
Kiss me and hold me
The sun and the flowers and the wind they all know
That I love you now and forever.

T, M, Thompson
July 4, 2001

Stars in the Sky

All around us and so near at hand
Is the truth waiting for us to discover
Like the stars at night that shine ever so bright
That are hiding there under a cover.

Under a cover of clouds, and behind city lights
Stars waiting for us to come see
Their beauty and majesty and distant worlds
And a view, of what's eternity.

For the sky we see and the sky we know
Is not the one that does really exist
But to us it becomes a reality
And upon its form we do insist.

A sky with a moon and a couple stars
Is the night that we see every day
But away from the crowds and the city
There awaits an incredible display.

There are millions of stars in the sky every night
For us there to look and enjoy
That can be seen from every country and region
By every man, every woman, and boy.

And so it is with regard to truth
It waits there for all to find
It only needs you to leave the old ways
And to open up your closed mind.

For ultimate truth is not hidden
It waits there for those wanting to know
In an age and a place and too in a time
When individuals and souls choose to grow.

So then realize that the stars in the night
And the city in which you now dwell
Are just a part of the reality of "All That There Is"
That exists between Heaven and Hell

There is so much more beyond all the clouds
Both those in the sky and your mind
So if you so choose you have nothing to lose
Go explore and enjoy what you'll find.

For each time and age needs explorers
Needs those willing to leave city and shore
Who can tell those who like to stay where they are
That beyond all the clouds there's much more.

T. M. Thompson
August 17, 2011

Gold Bread Water

A wise old man had a bag of gold
He also had a loaf of bread
His wisdom came from his experiences
And also from the things he'd read.

A student sat beside his feet
And said wise one please do tell
Which of all is the more important
The gold, the bread, or yon well.

The wise old man said it is none of these
For each in its time can give life
To the pauper the gold is what he would choose
To end both his lack and his strife.

To the starving man it would be the bread
For he craves neither the gold nor the water
But only for food for himself and his family
For his son, for his wife and his daughter.

And in the barren desert 'neath a burning sun
Worth much more than the gold is cool water
For the gold casts no shade nor quenches one's thirst
As the day becomes hotter and hotter.

And so it is with so many, many, things
That importance depends on one's need
To the poor it is money to the orphan it's love
To others it's power or greed.

And the wise old man also went on to say
That importance is like leaves on a tree
Changing and falling replaced every year
By new things you want and you see.

So know that importance forever does change
So compare not one thing to another
What's important to you means nothing to me
To your friend, your sister, or brother.

What's important is today and your happiness
And the reason for such you will find
Lies not in the world or the palm of your hand
But only from within your own mind.

T. M. Thompson
September 16, 2011

This poem begins will the thoughts of a soul preparing to incarnate. Most of what follows is from a poem I wrote for a contest many years ago. The requirement of the contest was that it be 2,500 to 3,000 words in length. The poem in its entirety is on my poetry website and is entitled, "A Time to Remember" written July 8, 1979.

Birth and Death

More and more do I remember less and less
More and more I am aware of the child I am to be
And more and more I remember my parents

Such fondness I have for these old friends
And with such warmth do I again remember
What it is like to have parents and be cradled in their arms
And in their thoughts.

More and more I can feel the blood in my veins
And hear my mother's breathing
More and more are there sights and sounds
Familiar yet new.

Familiar yet .....
But wait ...
Wait...

There is something else I remember
But the sounds of life do cloud my mind
My own quickening pulse cries out to me.

And now a thing to do
It is all that fills my mind
A thing to do
An urgency

A time arrived
Now.
Now.
Now.

Sounds and sights
I do not know
Sounds and sights
That come and go.
Father, mother
Table, chair
Some come here
And some go there.

Sleep and hunger
Things to hold
Warmth and mother
Dark and cold.

Move my head
And now my feet
Not well done
So I repeat.

Slowly learning
Right on course
This a dog
This a horse.

In my mind
I cannot say
Things I know
So ends my day

In the poem "A Time to Remember" there is a bridge between the preceding and the following stanzas which details the life of the child. Here my purpose is to show how a beginning can be so like the end. Each soul chooses the time and method of their departure. What I have written suggests to me a soul that has chosen their final method to incorporate the symptoms of Alzheimer's. The following stanzas are the thoughts of the child, now old, on the verge of death.

Sounds and sights
I do not know
Sounds and sights
That come and go.

Wife and brother
Table, chair
Some come here
And some go there.

Sleep and hunger
Things to hold
Warmth and shadows
Dark and cold.

Move my head
And now my feet
Not well done
So I repeat.

Keep forgetting
But of course
This a dog
And this a horse.

In my mind
I cannot say
Things I know
So ends my day.

T. M. Thompson
December 9, 2011

It is Time to Remember

The time approaches to be born once again
So I may continue to learn and to grow
The time approaches to enter illusion
And to take with me all that I know.

Like the times I was rich and the times I was poor
Or the time I was wise yet a fool
It's time to remember my lives as a drunk
And the lives where I was savage and cruel.

It is time to remember lives of great power
And being honored by all of my peers
It's time to remember lives of great courage
And the lives when I was shackled by fears.

It's time to remember my lives as a male
When I thought women were there just to be bred.
And it's time to remember my lives as a woman
Where I learned how to lead not be led.

It's time to remember my lives as a cripple
Where on others I had to depend
And it's time to remember my lives as a healer
When both body and souls I did mend.

It's time to remember those who killed me
And to remember all those whom I did slay
Knowing that on this stage we're only actors
And this illusion is only a play.

There were so many roles with such different goals
That I choose so I would finally awake
But now I am ready to be All That I Am
And happily the next step now will take.

For each incarnation I choose did thus change me
And now all purposes and lessons I see
Choosing now to be born and to now change the world
Instead of the world changing me.

For each soul as it grows is a student
Using illusion to learn what is true.
To finally arrive at a point at a place
Knowing what it is next they must do.

For there is never only one teacher
One Saint, one God or pure soul
But each of you arrive and at last to progress
To become teachers which is really the goal.

So those of you here that now read this
By the Law of Attraction you are all like me
Awakening to the knowledge of All That You Are
And becoming All That You Can Be.

Teachers to young souls and to seekers
Who know not that their stage is illusion
You guide and support all those encountered
To remove their limitations and confusion.

So congratulations then on your awakening
And I hope you enjoy your new role
As you nurture and guide those around you
As you enlighten and awaken each soul.

T. M. Thompson
December 7, 2011

Life, Love and Everything in Between: Poetry to Empower, Enlighten and Entertain Your Soul is an inspirational collection of poetry written by Terrence Thompson. The poems gathered in this volume span decades with some written as early as the 1970s and the most recent ones in 2011. Thompson writes about what inspires him. It might be a passing thought or something that a friend said, and then, the poet writes, the words and thoughts seem to flow. Many of his poems refer to nature and the elements or to reincarnation and thoughts about life, its purpose and the personal journey each person travels during their lifetime. Thompson speaks directly to his audience, whether it is the person who has influenced his writing or those unknown readers he envisions reading his words at some point in the future.

—Maggie

In his inspirational collection of poetry, Life, Love and Everything in Between: Poetry to Empower, Enlighten and Entertain Your Soul, Terrence Thompson shares so much of himself, his life and his perceptions. Reading this book of verse is a heady experience with the poet a seasoned and sometimes nostalgic guide who, every so often, will interject a bit of play or irreverence to make sure his audience doesn't take him or themselves too seriously. His discussions of faith and his take on it are enlightening and never presume to lead or influence, though I did notice in one poem that he casts a mildly jaundiced yet tender eye at a friend's belief in karmic punishment. Thompson's verses flow naturally with rhymes that seem comfortable and fitting, but my favorite poem in this collection would have to be the predominantly free verse work entitled Reflections. It was in that poem that somehow I heard the poet's voice most clearly. Life, Love and Everything in Between is highly recommended.

—Jack